The Magic of What's There

David Morley won the Ted Hughes Award for New Poetry in 2016 for *The Invisible Gift: Selected Poems* and a Cholmondeley Award for his contribution to poetry. His collections include *The Gypsy and the Poet*, a PBS Recommendation and Morning Star Book of the Year; *Enchantment*, a Sunday Telegraph Book of the Year; *The Invisible Kings*, a PBS Recommendation and TLS Book of the Year. A dramatic long poem, *The Death of Wisdom Smith, Prince of Gypsies*, has been published by The Melos Press. He is Professor at Warwick University and Monash University, Melbourne.

T0167886

The Magic
of What's There

David Morley

CARCANET

First published in Great Britain in 2017
by Carcanet Press Ltd
Alliance House, 30 Cross Street,
Manchester M2 7AQ
www.carcanet.co.uk

A CIP catalogue record for this book is available
from the British Library, ISBN 9781784104948

Book design: Luke Allan. Printed & bound
in England by SRP Ltd. The publisher acknowledges financial
assistance from Arts Council England.

Contents

to Brenda Tomlinson
and in memory of Charles Tomlinson

I The Discovery

I quam a Quunnock

and in this moment
    moment's minion

        a fledgling
           dunnock

      sky-dives
        through

     the open door
of my writing shed

      catches itself crossly
          in my hair

          crash-lands crabbily
            on the keyboard

        fleetingly
       pressing

      the letter Q –
       tweeting

          # I quam
            a QUUNNOCK!

            # I QUAM QUITING
              A QUOEM!

The Grace of JCBs

Spring detonates on time thanks to wood anemones.
Woodland is wan without a million of them.

JCBs squat on fly-blown, gull-flocked hills.
They are King of Rat and glory to the gulls.

Wood anemones slink through crumbs of soil,
heads bowed by darkness, darkness limned by toil.

JCBs shovel rancid rubbish over tilth.
They rule by ramming everything in sight.

Anemones explode like stars or solar flare.
They glow and glister on the forest floor.

JCBs chew up tonnage and spit out filth.
Magpies choose their JCB and stick by *him*.

Wood anemones shift sidelong to the sun.
Their shoots are metronomes in slow emotion.

Rooks erupt in raptures around a JCB.
Their Midas, Grail, their Holy of Holies.

Wood anemones harvest ultraviolet rays.
Early bees are drawn droning to their gaze.

Nothing saddens a JCB more than a stalled JCB.
He ploughs across the planet to hold him, steady.

The lives of wood anemones are swift. We hail
their fleet and fleetness, their golden crisis.

JCBs squat on fly-blown, bird-flocked hills.
Spring detonates on time, thanks to JCBs.

Dr Seuss Passes through the Gates of Heaven

you came to a place where   the streets were not marked
some windows were lighted   but mostly they're darked

and you heard a song   rise over the snow
it started in low   then it started to grow

now your snow is all white
now your work is all done

now your house is all right
i will not let you fall

i will hold you up high
as i stand on a ball

with a book in one hand
and a cup on my hat

now   now
have no fear   have no fear

said
the Cat

The blue whale's heart is a four-chambered car

A zebra fish suffers a broken heart? He grows another
while octopi, like queens, are blue-blooded with copper.

Earthworms host five hearts; the cuttlefish, three.
A bee's heart runs down the length of one bee.

A hibernating hedgehog's heart beats five times
to my minute's seventy-two. Every beat rhymes.

Naked Poem

to Django Bennett-Clarke, a boy with Type 1 Diabetes
from his friend, David, with Type 1 Diabetes

In Edward's Lane in Worcestershire,
a green lane slunk across by Bow Brook.

Despite being the swansong of an English summer,
it was a puzzle to find a way across

or in the hedgerow gain a path aground
and through or over that slown ford.

Your mum writes to me about the boy she adores:
Django loves to run, full speed! When he feels himself

going high he gets up and exercises around the sofa
at breakneck speed, or around the garden, or down

the hills, or bounces repeatedly on the bed coming up
with 'new groovy jumps', the pump a part of his body.

Godspeed and birdsong and tramping
the Australian bush; waterfalls climbed at dawn

solo, with a sugar rush; rain forests rent
by the rattles of kookaburras; canopies

cackling with rosellas... I flew home,
my mind lit by the fling of lorikeets,

puffed parrots, curled koalas,
the flit and flirt of honeyeaters.

Injections greet both dawn and dusk, and birdsong.
Django, I have never felt less afraid. Of life.

The Discovery

of graphene, University of Manchester, 2004

'It's like the Large Hadron Collider, but on your desktop.'
ANDRE GEIM

A single sheet of graphene being one atom thick,
sufficient in size to cover a football pitch,

would weigh under one single gram. Like graphene
a poem's girder-strong yet essentially unseen,

a singing mesh more sinew than structural steel.
Andre Geim once levitated a frog and wrote a paper

with his hamster. Geim and friend Novoselov were
at play in his laboratory; that day with graphite

and Scotch tape, gaming with science and art
on their worktop while Manchester stood stone-still.

Patience and slow exfoliation of atom-thick layers...
What art was there, when they stripped the mineral strata

and the poetry opened before them as atoms?
And atoms and atoms unfurled in a singing mesh.

II   *Husbandry*

Mercy

Charles Tomlinson in Ozleworth

Charles spoons a sip of honey
on the proboscis of a downed

bumblebee, slips an upended glass
around that arse-tipped buzzing

fuzz-ball, and palms a wisp
of paper fast beneath.

The bee revs and side-slips,
learning to lift the head-butting,

humming helicopter of herself.
She steadies astride her parcels

of pollen. Charles's fingertips
fizz as her rotors race; raises

the guarding glass and the bee
rises resurrected from the grass.

Husbandry

When I was a baby, my mum planted a row
of four baby apple trees at the foot of our garden.

She winter-washed the saplings scrupulously.
In March mum slapped and bound grease tight around

to daunt caterpillars inching to the leaves.
Infant trees arose and poured pinked blossom

each apple-flower cross-pollinating.
Charles Ross. Laxton Superb and Fortune. Beauty of Bath.

I grew with these trees at the same height each year.
When I reached seven, mum took pruning shears

to them and sealed the dribbling sap with tar.
This wounding only spurred a spurt of growth.

Next year the trees began pumping out apples.
I was drawn by their blossom's scent each April

the moment that they budded on the boughs.
They seemed to burst from bud to fruit overnight.

The lure for a child was to pluck and bite
those tart infant apples before they swelled;

there were casualties by gall and codling moth
or fruit pecked putrid by blackbird or thrush.

To hide my thefts I took only babies,
marble-like, equally, from each of the trees.

I prayed for gales. Windfalls were treasure.
In September we took them in their season.

Salted to drive out bugs; dried in the violet
of the sun's antibiotic, buffed to a glow

then stowed in old newspaper for winter
in cardboard boxes under our parents' bed.

*   *   *   *   *   *

Dad would lodge one apple in his pocket
when he left early for the industrial estate.

The rest were put to play: on Halloween,
the children of the house would bob for them

(the apple being the prize). On Christmas Eve
they wound their way into toes of stockings,

scented by Laxton Fortune's insulin tang,
past perfume of their being once alive.

By Easter, the boxes under the bed were bare.
Dad started dying in the eighth year

of the apples. Customs of cancer-care
could not cease mum's raising of her trees.

Winter-washing; grease-banding; pollinating;
spraying; harvesting; pruning; tarring;

salt-cleansing; sun-drying; stowing; boxing.
Every act a clear concentrating.

The trees thrived. They began to improve on
my springing height because of her attention.

By the day dad was cremated, the trees
were out of control. My older brother

was also out of control. We lived in fear.
His arrest brought silence and a truce

because now it was only me and mum,
my sister having grown up and gone.

And the trees had grown beyond us both.
August was florid with a yield so vast

apples thudded sluggishly on slug-slick grass.
Blackbirds and thrushes, worms, larvae.

One tree's care could take one longish day
and I was a teenager, 'father of the house'.

Late-December, while they slept under snow
she hacked their trunks then tore the taproots free.

'They were too much bother.' She turned over
their bones in the snow-fire and stared past me

along the opened graves of her four trees.

Innocence

Who was my uncle but a man who'd stoop
to earthworms stranded on streets after showers;

ply those panicky squiggles softly,
their clitella pulsing between calloused

thumb, forefingers, settling them safely,
innocents, or innocence, among grass.

Lesson Three

Dad was not dad. Dad was the mad train
screaming daily into the station of his home,

white-hot brakes shrieking, exploding across
the platforms of the rooms. So regular,

so on time, you could set your watch. Five hours.
Four. Three. Two. The skies were my watch.

I saw the evening redden, and I hid.
Hiding to nowhere. A phrase I still hate.

Dad's train shivered and splintered the front door.
He would steam home and hit me for being

home. If he didn't hammer me, he'd waltz
on toys with his work-boots and kick the wreckage

in my face. Then he'd stamp on my fingers.
I'd dive under the bed to save my hands.

Lego. He'd grind Lego to smithereens.
A hiding. That's the toy he brought home.

When I was six, I hid inside a bottle
of corked cooking brandy. Passed out cold. *Ten*:

his train tore through the walls, screeched
to a halt at the buffers of the prone boy.

You're fucking pissed, he hissed, smiling. He chugged on
on on, leaving soot and sweat all over my skin.

But I'd dodged a beating. Slight strategy.
I'd even cheered him. That was Lesson One.

Lesson Two was not to speak. Not to exhale
one white word. Silence starved the furnace.

Dad's coal-heart cindered. The steel face flickered,
lit lightly, pistons heaving on heavy wheels.

Huff Huff as his engine snored on its sleepers.
There were no more trains that night.

*　　　*　　　*　　　*　　　*　　　*

Hiding. Not speaking. Habits grafting
to a character that's there, that's not there –

that shared dad's table, hearth, his suddy bath
each Sunday night; and knew never, never,

never to speak or show or point or tell
or mind or feel or think, or stare. Or steal.

I stole silence. I stole hushed thunder.
Trains could come and go. Ghost trains at night.

Rippety-trip-rippety-trip. I fell.
I fell over my tongue. Or my tongue tripped

over me. At school I had spoken, read
aloud, sang in assembly. *Teacher's pet*,

my brother spat (he, a half-slid train
off the rails). Silence then: then a stammer.

Nothing between or beyond. No straight sound.
All strained. Nictitating. Reined.

Dad's train steamed, fumed, fretted beside its platform.
I could hear him grinding along the rails

of loft-rafters at night. He would half-slide
my bedroom door open, in the sidings

of dark. But the boiler blew up in him.
Dad's lungs were smoked-out. They hung with tumours

thick with soot. He coughed like a strangling:
throttled, mouthing, mantling over a bucket,

over boltings of spew. I'd take that light-blue bucket,
flush the stuff, sluice it; kneel once more beneath

his retching, ravaged, wrought-apart chest, almost like I
was waiting. Waiting for him to get some steam up.

To explode. Through the walls. So I said nothing.
The sick, the dying. They can say anything.

*   *   *   *   *   *

The Juvenile Court, Fleetwood, 1979.
My *So sorry* speech so slowly rehearsed

for hours to a mirror, my brother banging
and banging on the bathroom door: *Will you*

fucking well stop yakking to yourself!
Stranded in the dock, fish-stench from the Docks

offal-pungent until the trawlers dry-docked
in the Cod War. I fell over my tongue. Or

my tongue fell over me. I had to tilt at it.
To sound like thirteen-year-old truth.

I realise I have done wrong. I am sorry
for my actions. I promise never to do this again.

How far did I get? *I re—   I re—   I re— !*
(then higher, panicking) *I RE— !* My brother

was snorting, pissing himself. The young judge
gazed over his glasses, mystified, encouraging.

His slight kindness turned the tap – words. Words, like w—
w— w— *w— w— w—* W— W— W —*WATER*

shot out as if hosed, splattering meaning
in the dropping well of conscience.

'What did you say?' – the judge leans forward. 'I re—?'
I am not sorry to tell you I'm not sorry.

Am I lying? I'm not lying. This was Lesson Three.

II   The Field Guide

Wheatear

We kneel by a dry-stone wall. The bird flies closer.
It is as if neither of us tried seeing before.

'Whinchat?' you ask, touching my arm, 'or wheatear?'
The field guide flickers under one finger.

Somewhere, it says, between a robin and blackbird.
Somewhere between a hawfinch and fieldfare.

We are trying to imagine a winged shape. But look.
Look at the bird. It has forgotten the air.

It darts in front of us. It warps and flicks its plumes:
brown, black, white, blue, grey, gold. The wheatear

preens, snatches stoneflies, dances over moss cushions,
stitches a nest-cup between heavens of heather.

Try, as if no one had ever tried before,
to say what you see, feel, love, lose.

Gravity

after the Anglo-Saxon

Your palms are wan. Your eyes are streams.
    You stare a pit into the ground in dream.

        I offer this heart-cure: carline thistle,
            stamens of iris, yew-berry, lupine,

        elecampane, marshmallow head,
    fen-mint, dill, lily, cock's-spur grass,

penny royal, horehound, dock,
    elder, earth-gall, wormwood,

        strawberry leaves, comfrey;
          mix these with well-water

        then sing this charm three times over:
    I have wrapped my love with invisible bonds

So its injury neither stirs nor seethes,
    Nor spreads through my body, nor festers

        In my soul; nor the wound wax beyond its walls,
          Nor the entry wound spill; nor the exit wound seal.

        For we must bleed freely over the field,
        For we must hold our hearts to the sun.

Nor feel it more than the earth feels the moon.

Lorca, an Apparition

Just once I heard it rive the night,
arrow the air with a wire thread

– an owl's gaze made visible. I said
to my friends how I longed to hear it

a song for gone centuries, a wretched
resurrection of love under other worlds

and other moons and other winds.
A scream from the sum of our dead.

Lorca heard the siguiriya of gypsies
tear love apart with a scream that slices –

tear life apart with a scream that slices –
the earth into two trembling hemispheres.

Hassle

The man who has not the whip-hand of his tongue
and temper is not fit to go into company but Mike

is Mike is Mike, and all's thrown from horizon to sky
when his whip-hand's wired by White Lightning and Rye.

That is how we imagine him. Unfit for human society.
Mike thinks the planet's one long bloody hassle.

Constellations spinning in the wing-mirror of his van
whether police cars or pole stars Mike's heading home

to the full beam of a haulage depot, the sump and spill
of his caravan site, to the tilted mirror of a bottle,

the windscreen smash of hangover, to the oil chamber
of lawyers' chambers, the handbrake turn of high court,

wheel spins of reporters. The exhaust of exhaustion
after hours haggling and hustling over access to his children.

Migration

And you turn the bird hide inside-out
as if the birds, not us, inhabited it

and it is they, the birds, staring,
making a count, noting the rings

at our ankles, plumage, predation,
our massed, amassed migratory pattern;

and they fed us through winter,
placed wooden boxes for us to inter

our families, observed our mating
annually through motion-activated

cameras, their beaks, their little eyes
at the windows of the hide's eyes.

We'd stand dumb in our flock, stare back
at them, world's weather at our back.

IV Sycamore Bark

Red Spider Mite

Tetranychus urticae

i empty
my pockets

of small stones
and make

my minuscule
spider mite thrones

red emperors
in your scarlet

country
i watch you

through the
lifelong day

wishing myself
in your

miniature
physiology

free not to
be free

the feel of not to
feel it

After a Song by Gustav Mahler

Love teaches you how to mind
and how to mend. Love teaches you

how to hold your breath and hold
a wreath. It does not teach you how

to breathe nor how to live through
life alone. Love shows you must learn.

A Spectrogram by Messiaen

Lapwings gyre and jape,
their plunging love

a thrumming, swerving
spirographing dive.

A Duet by Schubert

Slender alders lift
and lilt in the squall,

serenading one another
or nothing at all.

Sycamore Bark

from letters between Paul Celan and Nelly Sachs

'But the healing happens on a new path for way in and way out can never be the same when farewell and reunion are parted by the incurable wound of life and the aura of early morning is the answer and gift...'
Letter from Nelly Sachs to Paul Celan, June 1961

'Heather and centaury, honeysuckle

and foxglove and broom brush.
We know we can and may rely on you.'

We know you will bring us no word
from the wound of knowing that it may never.

That it may never, in all binds, yield colour,
be bee-blessed, flower, become becoming, be.

I cannot turn from you, or you from me,
though we turn, torn, draw breath, free.

I draw an arrow and shoot it at the tree.
I cannot see where it struck. I cannot see.

I cannot hear what the wound sings to me:
the honeysuckle, heather and centaury.

The foxglove and the broom brush.

The foxglove and the broom brush:

'I can see that the net is still there,
it can't be taken away by a wave of the hand',

or release the trapped, turning butterfly
writhing in the web her wing-beats ply.

Alarm. Acceptance. Silence. No god
who would not stir to lift you, gently,

from where you are snared,
limed. Hairstreak Butterfly.

No mercy that would not clasp, invisibly,
palms under the stained glass of your wings.

Impossibly its net is still there. It can't
be taken away by a wave of the hand.

In the white May night I write this.

'In the white May night I write this

    for I cannot sleep' – Spring scribbles
    like an infant: woodpecker drums and drills;

    talons stretch, clench; chicks bicker
    in nest-cups snagged on hawthorn.

    The year wakes raw, cawing softly.
    May's white days stern with sunlight

    straighten stem, stalk, skeletal stamen,
    bowed heads taken in hand by sunlight.

    Chatter of the beck. Divining dippers.
    Clattering routs of grouse. Rustling deer.

    Wild flowering rattles of aquilegia
    wake in a high field of gold and water

from a dream of wintering without air.

Dream of singing without air or exemplar.

    The laboratory goldfinch, orphaned as a chick
    takes a singing lesson from air: to screech,

    to scream air (no lesson lessens less)...
    Celan to Sachs: 'I inhale your work

    when I go to rest in the evening.
    It lies beside me on the table' – words

    as air; song as songster; wren trill, wren;
    murmuration, purely flock dynamics.

    Imagine a choir of, a choir.
    Aria and air, song to singer –

    impossibility impossibly possible –
    uppermost starling-mote chasing the lower:

one impossibly possible without the other.

Impossibly possible: a meridian of pain and comfort –

Sachs to Celan: 'If only the gold would again
come through the air out of the mystery'.

Celan to Sachs: 'Poems, and yours especially,
are even better pieces of sycamore bark'.

Sachs to Celan: 'After the departure and then
being drawn through the air and then to step

out, torn away – but you had hurried before me'.
'What a joy, the glass window, your letter,

the sycamore bark'. God, who would not stir
to lift us from this field of gold and water –

'with the ancient light on its brow
and the heart the manacled fugitive

leaps for its calling: to be a wound—'

I draw an arrow and shoot it at the tree.

    I cannot hear what that wound sings to me.
    'It has been black for us both so long, I felt

    for you through countries... Paul, dear Paul,
    if a little gold came to me from nowhere

    upon my heart I would send it to you.'
    I could not turn from you, or you from me,

    be bee-blessed, flower, become becoming, be.
    It would never, in all binds, yield colour –

    though we turned, torn, drew breath, free.
    'For your lines, for the reminder of that light.'

    'I have always carried you in my heart.'
    'All gladness, dear Nelly, all light!'

I drew an arrow and drove it into me.

V Forgiveness

Bipolarity, an Eroded Pantoum

o but he has turned   worship this whorl of him

    why is that mountain   we were   walking on
    a collapsed world   i can   strike through
    searching for his step   among   stung grass
where is that mountain   we   were   hiking upon
    i fill my pockets   with stalled stones
search for his step   among rushes   or mosses
of   five   streams   we crossed   together
    i fill   my pocket   with eroded stones
    that i   might   place them   before me
    five streams we   crossed re-crossed
this river flickered its flow   talks to or through stones
    that i might   place   those stones before me
    read   his   erosions   in fresh- lorn light
    it flickered do i talk   to myself in stone
    now i   stare on   the river- smoothed bed
read   that sheering   in fresh-lorn light
collapsed   worlds   I can stare through them
    now   I stare   on this river's   ruined   stones
is turned all stone   all stone eroded   this whorl of him

51

A Sad Tale's Best for Winter

MAMILLIUS: There was a man –
Dwelt by a churchyard: I will tell it softly;
Yond crickets shall not hear it.

The Winter's Tale: II, I

I am like you, they say. A prince. A son.
They say I pined for mother, that her shame

shrunk my heart to a husk and blood's wind
blew me hollow. Believe me, I am no fool

nor a poet of such precise, nameable griefs.
Harm is set and struck like a fuse. I could not grow old.

Mother passed me like a parcel to her ladies,
a trouble, past enduring. I was her worn son

yet I won her wonder with soft-spoken stories,
her eyebrows arched, her irises widened: *fright me*

with your sprites, she would say, *you're powerful at it.*
A sad tale's best for winter, I whispered, *I have one.*

I fuelled father with flatteries yet my bowels
were water. I watched him count the coins

of my years then stack them, weeping:
I lost a couple, that 'twixt heaven and earth

might thus have stood begetting wonder...
Pray now, for with mere conceit

and fear of the queen's speed, I was gone.
I am not like you, you see. I was their son.

Forgiveness

'Do not imagine I put you there / for nothing.'
W. S. Graham, 'Imagine a Forest'

i.

```
    leaf  and tree      try       for their first   flower
 it has  taken        millennia         to bring  life  to pass
  spectra  of sunlight   astray   seeds   among  grass
 their  white child      blossoms    for a     single  hour


   leaf  blames  tree    tree   blames  the  mother
  roots   tremble in beds   listening     to them brawl
  tree  screams at  leaf      leaf  shrieks at   soil
  roots    cannot    tell      father  from    mother


  all  winter  tree        nursed  infant  leaf
 last  autumn's leaves        died      incarnadine
come spring  tree  tells her    you  will  wear  my  crown
 tree   is   unfurling  this   lie     all    his   life


   branches wrestle for   a  boy's  snagged    kite
  roots   wrangle    underground in  tests  of  length
     tree drags water up a  well  of  his  strength
 leaf is trying to  be  life    yet   nothing  is    right


 tree's canopy susurrates      'we    may   not   die'
 that   leaf  makes  tree      that  tree  makes grief
 that   root and  branch       shall never  know  leaf
    except  they  will        for  all  trees   lie


 roots   rise  to  their   tip      toes  in  spate  as  it rains
   drought is  white  spite     tree   is   past  caring
    he   stabs  into   soil   steals water    swearing
   you  have nothing  to  lose but  your  daisy  chains
```

53

two   late   leaves   condemned   to   downfall
they   cling   conjoined   they   clamour   for life
branch   suckles   seedlings   scarcely   in   leaf
a   trapdoor   bangs   open   and   that   is   all

behold   a   king's   canopy   tree   cries   to   sunset
holds   high   his   crown   drinks   in   all   earth
behind   every   great   tree   is   a   great   leaf   stutters leaf
roots   rant   in   the   dark: *the   death   of   trees   is   a   silhouette*

tree's   mass   executions   erupt   in   autumn
leaf   lifts   her   meek   heads   to   the   hatchet   of   winds
if   tree   truly   wanted   to   forgive   our   sins
then   why   did   not   tree   just   forgive   them

haloes   of   tree   rings   ignite   under   bark
veins   of   xylem   swell   with   blossom and   birdspring
tree   awakes   awakens   to   an   ice-   blast   of   song
leaf   light   flickers   on   wands   in   the   dark

tree: *grief   makes   you   see   things   that   are   not   there*
leaf: *teach   me   to   breathe   by   holding   to   the   sun*
to hold   *to leaf*
beyond   *the   grief*   *of autumm*

Winter, after Winter

Everything is mathematics, impenetrable
in an ache of algorithms and cat's-cradles;

as everything is played and patterned
in arrangements that tally the arrays

of tines on a pine cone: that living grenade
– that grenade, that little, bristling bomb

quietly released into seed-dispersing form.
Look! A Crossbill dangles by her talons.

She tugs out paper-like seeds effortlessly.
How adapted she is for struggle. Her bill

twists in two directions, one against the other.

Outside these stern woods she could not thrive.

She would be mocked, mobbed and alone.
She would be crowned clown among birds.

Half her face is scissor, the other stone.
Mangled, ripped apart, crippled by the cold,

the pine cone flinches from the Crossbill's scythe.
The whole tree tilts one way by the wind

but the thing clings. Blizzards rip in. Polar dawns
drain the Crossbill's thermal core and the tree's

sap crawls then freezes. Winter after winter
they tear life from each other. To the end of days.

VI The Teardrop Stoop

Yarak

*Eastern term for when a hunting bird's training, weight
and mental focus all comes together in the field*

In

a soar

a peregrine looks

like a toy bird kite;

in a glide, her shape brings

to mind a drawn bow. In a stoop,

the wings are finely folded so that the

falcon mimics a missile. In a teardrop stoop

the falcon may pump her wings to accelerate, or

the wings may be completely clasped against her body

so that the bird is shaped like a teardrop. A peregrine passes

a falling skydiver as if the skydiver were standing still. From the

view of the sky-diver the falcon is invisible. A stooping peregrine

can trick the mind – of a man, of a pigeon – into thinking the bird has

cloaked. Preying peregrine falcons plunge through the sky at more than

250 miles per hour, levelling at the last minute to strike speeding pigeons

in an explosion of feathers. The peregrine outflies her vision: diving faster than

her brain can process – the peregrine flies blind. A pigeon has evolved to home in

on the sound of the stooping cloaked falcon. Pigeons warp one wing and roll

out of the falcon's path. From the view of a falcon, she is flying at top speed

toward the back of the pigeon, fervently fixed on its tail. White feathers

under the tail, flicked upwards on attack, flicker to disguise the start

of the evasive roll, confusing the attacker with sudden contrast

between the conspicuous white flare of feathering and a

grey-blue body. Such is the momentary loss of vision

lasting no more than $1/50^{th}$ of a second, the falcon

under-compensates her strike as if she

led her gun's sight ahead of her prey.

White-tailed deer, scuts of rabbits,

sandpipers, quick-silvering fish

alternate displays of dark and

light surfaces to confuse

predators. They have

thrown falcons and

scientists from

planes to test

this.

59

The Teardrop Stoop

Teardrop *(verb): To stoop downwards in a teardrop shape.*
Stoop *(verb): To tuck in the wings and dive headfirst from a height*
TERMS OF FALCONRY

Amok mocking tercels slide-fly, gangling
on creances, crabbing over catches,

mantling offal, blood-booted in raw cruor.
The falcon rakes away from her spun prey,

pulls out of her stoop, foiled by cacophony.
Grounded birds are rounded up, gauntleted,

handled to their hawk-boxes, the free-lofts.
The whirling lure blandishes her: this bechin,

this gift of grume, this Catherine-wheeling
quarry: chick, wood-mouse – this neck-nipped tempter.

Tracker, trailer, trapper, her talons unsheathed –
fore-swept, dead-locked, whetted, teardropped to stoop –

strikes the lure – mid-air, mid-arc – clasps, clenches
its crushed coils; lays over, sunning on her sharps.

I knew her first as a brancher, pin-feathered,
gawky, mewing for tidbits, daughtered

to a haggard; she, strafed by hunger streaks.
I cast the bird to cope her, cere to beak;

imped her of fret marks, fastened fresh coverts,
as she sloughed, shook, side-stepped her blood feathers.

Intermewed, enseamed, she bobbed and bated
on her block perch. Penned-hard, she bloomed,

bowsed and bathed in her mews. Full summed
in flight feathers, wrangling for hours with a tiring

while tercels bickered, covetous, hungering
through the chicken wire of her hawk-dwelling.

What were tercels when she had widgeon wing?
She mantled over raw meat, fleshed herself strong.

She weathers with Lannerets and Sakarets –
blind emperors in turbaned Turk's Head Knots –

bound, jessed, sunned, flumped upon their parched perches
in the weathering yard. Tercels bathe and bowse,

feak, vomit, ruffle, preen, tug up talons
of one foot, wing-over their ceres, and doze.

Sole Falcon among males, she snites, swivels
and vents; warbles her wings above her back

tenting tensioned sarcels. *Falco peregrinus*
full-roused, her bow-perch both eye and eyrie,

raking the sun-wan yawning yard for quarry.
Rankling, mantling, muting, slicing – in sheer

yarak of her yearning; casting off from the fist
of the hunt, gyring to her sky-eyed pitch.

She has done with tiring, that too tough gobbet
of rabbit, crop-crunched, rangled with gravel,

endewed to the stomach before casting.
Now for her grace-grooming: her beak trawling

remiges, rectrices, pendants, alula,
her preen gland gleaming. She stipples her beak,

tongues oils over and between rachis, vane,
barbs, sarcels, down, crural, calamus,

semi-plumes, filo-plumes. Self-touch soothes her.
Soft-eyed, she ruffles. She shuffles over.

I caress her commissure with one finger.
She rocks on her keel, downily, drowsily.

Are we daring each other? I draw the braces
of her hood so that they tauten and clasp.

She springs in her yarak, ripe in her crouch.
I slip an anklet around her tarsus,

jesses to make her bracelet, snug bewit
for her bells. She binds to my wrist, warbling,

bobbing before casting off, sprung, free-flying,
stamps stairs of air, punching breeze, flinging

thumped thermals; vectors, vortices whistling,
isthmi of force fountaining, bouncing

beneath her aimed, armed anti-grav sheer through
cirrrus, stratus, woolpacks of cumulus;

eclipsing, outcropping, playing the plinth
of her pitch, two thousand feet above my stare.

                    She stalls over the lure –
                        stoops.

Rock–climbs Remembered for their Perfumes

CRYSTAL SLABS, PEMBROKESHIRE

Grass-of-Parnassus.
        Fringecups. Fingertips

of saxifrage clinging
        to limestone scarps:

I stare down flowerheads as if
        clambering into their open mouths,

a pollinator scenting by tongue
        the nectars beneath their tongues,

above their white necks
        between their white lips

– not clean-white,
        those fingering petals,

but veined with lucent
        jade stripes cupped

around a wasp's crown of stamens;
        climbing through, wary not

to garden the crag but to leave
        bare stone clear.

Cloudberry flower high
            on Aonach Eagach: a sly, sky-

white hour scrambling
            in a sunned daze

of ropes, chocks and tapes
            to the toe of some eyrie

of an arête; then scissoring
            the ridge in a surge

before the problems pile
            down like smirr

or a missed route;
            running empty

on electrolyte; cramming
            moss in your mouth

for its few tears
            of clenched mizzle;

clawing cloudberries
            from their stems for an atom's

burst of water,
            their tang of stung rain.

CNEIFION ARÊTE, GLYDER FAWR

for Siobhan Keenan

Ling: straggling
                  on every grab and ledge;

holding breath in heather's
                  swarming scent as if

to knock you down for a dare;
                  as if their heads breathed bees,

each buzzer with a jab
                  for your grasp as you haul

up through scratch-
                  your-eyes-out stems

as if flowers were
                  more spike than flower

roots more
                  razor than roots;

yet when the holds run
                  out, when the clean rock

teeters to throw you
                  around or about,

clutch them close-to
                  like dearest hair,

then your heather heads
                  are heaven-scent.

VII   A Second Life

The Crowd

for the 96

And today, as you walk to the match, I am beside you.
Proud to be alive. Proud to be walking beside you,

to take our seats together.
And you know my name. You know all our names.

We are beside and between you,
our souls, invisibly visible.

We are waking. We are smiling.
We are walking in your hearts.

And we are prouder still to know today,
tomorrow, next week, month or year

you will not chant us down again.
You will not chant us back into the earth.

For we left the earth where we thought we were alone
yet we are beside you, laughing and singing and unbroken.

If you were to hear me among the crowd
you would hear a song.

Were I to pass invisibly among your jostling arms,
or carried to earth, you would hear me singing with you.

If I took you to one side and told you 'you were my brother',
what would you sing to your brother?

If I took you to one side and told you 'you were my sister',
what would you sing to your sister?

You are my brother and you are my sister.
Nothing can kill me. I am the crowd.

*   *   *   *   *   *

And the sun shone over Merseyside, over Manchester,
over the Pennines with its skylarks and brightening becks,

over Penistone and Stocksbridge and Hillsborough.
Liverpool fans in their buses – cheering the roof off –

anticipation, faith in the day and the song of life
no stronger than your own, just scousier.

You will not chant them down again.
You will not chant them down in their sorrows.

You will not chant them back into the earth.
And today, as you walk to the match, they are beside you.

Proud to be walking beside you, to take your seats together.
And you know their names. You know all their names.

We are walking to the same match.
We are walking on the same road.

We are arriving at the same gates.
We are waiting. We are laughing. We are singing.

And we do not know it but this is joy.
Nothing can kill us. We are the crowd.

Night Flight

for Charles Tomlinson

Lunar Moths slip from their sleeping cradles
antennae addled, numbed from a night's candles

to tremble over mirrors in scorched spirals,
secreting flash colognes to flickering lovers.

Drab charismatics. Their wings are pommelled
as if soldered fastidiously then trammelled:

their night flight flows from dusk to dawn.

Their night flights flow from dusk to dawn:

the Powdered and Common Quakers have flown,
then the Delicates, the Wainscots and the Uncertains,

the Bright Waves, the Bricks and the Umbers,
Clouded Drabs, Neglected Rustics and Dusky Sallows,

the Great Brocades, Festoons and The Shears
through bloom of their dead perfumes, and hawthorn flowers.

Seven Springs of Ozleworth

for Brenda Tomlinson

Seven heavens of streams flowing to the Severn;
  so we flowed – we three – beside their under-heaven

of yellow-cress, water forget-me-not, asphodel,
  of sweet-flag, mare's tail, kingcup, English bluebell…

'*spr*' said the map seven times – so seven voices sprang:
  seven notes spilling, spiralling, harmonising

where Adam, Eden, Arden – and we three – ran together
  and Time itself beat to the cadence of the rivers.

In Malvern Woods

for Edward and Gabriel

We walk half knowing just how long we've got
to compass the dark, the still-point of the car.

My sons go quiet as an owl glides low.
We tread dead leaves into the forest floor.

They hate these walks until we're on the go
then they throng the woodland with unseen foes.

Enemies trounced, my children fall on me.
Joining in, I die or I pretend to die.

They know nothing of death except it's dumb
so offer up a second life to me.

I falter to my feet, faking a wound
and they, now serious, ask if I'm alright.

Not all is right, but that is where it ends.

Coda

The Way In

They're still alight, those enchanted streetlamps
between Little Malvern and Great Malvern.

There are chains of them beneath British Camp
bobbing like scuts of gas at twilight.

Lamps peter up the hillside to the wells
and flicker half visibly behind bare oaks

out-blazed by headlights of delivery trucks
shrieking through gears on drives of high hotels.

Those lamp-lanes are Christmas to my boys
at any dusk or in any season.

Winter days nod and the short light goes.
I read them stories as those low lamps glow.

Their dreams will line the lanes with Narnians.
The way in takes them running through the snow.

Stepping Stones

As we placed those seven stepping stones –
brashy bricks from a bramble-toppled wall –

the quick brook slackened her prattling chatter.
We heard her bottle-necked water bicker

against our fresh steps, prone to what water
knew, or had known for secret seasons –

gravel, sand, bedrock, her kingfishering
freshet swollen swift after the March thaw.

Leaf-surprised sunlight struggled on her sheen.
We had broken in, it seemed, on her privacy.

The water nagged and fretted around our stones
as if the brook were done considering our toil.

Now silently she drowned our little day
stone by stone by stone by stone by stone.

Bluebells for Edward and Gabriel

They are too few.
Beneath the evergreen yew
they broke through with the dew.

We'd glimpsed their hue
from the car as we flew
through Warwickshire woods, overdue.

By May they were new.
By June they are hewn.

But for you two (I name you)
April-shower-soaked-through –
they are for you. They are all for you.

Over the forest floor they strew
another sky,
as blue.

The Bell

Waiting for our children outside their school
I ask this stranger some foolish question
thinking my words the kind of thing a man
says to another father, believing
all fathers' lives approximate my own.

He replies but I am barely listening.
High sea. A squall. An overwhelmed dinghy.
Toys, nappies, straggling in its wake.
I look past him stupidly. I do not speak.

From where I stand he should have struck me down.
Of course he doesn't, and the school bell rings.
Staring through him I search only for my own.

And all our children run into the rain.

Leamington Bird Reserve Hide

The bird reserve is reedy and neglected
with drab posters of species in the hide.

At least, they seem like birds. With graffiti,
you wouldn't want your children to look closely.

Stubbed cigarettes scar the shelf where you place
your elbows as you lift binoculars.

My boys are seven and ten and unaware
all the little windows have been shattered.

Before them is their mind-made Serengeti:
crowned cranes, impalas, aardwolves... sycamores

spring with vervet and colobus monkeys.
The hide door bangs and bangs but they don't care.

Heat-haze stirs with steenboks and klipspringers.
We might as well make magic of what's there.

Notes

WHEATEAR '...try to say what you see and feel and love and lose' – Rainer Maria Rilke, *Letters to a Young Poet*

THE DISCOVERY Discoverer of graphene Andre Geim made headlines in 1997 when he used a magnetic field to levitate a frog, garnering him an IgNobel Prize in 2000. He co-authored a paper with his favourite hamster, *Detection of earth rotation with a dia-magnetically levitating gyroscope*, insisting that 'H.A.M.S. ter Tisha' contributed to the levitation experiment 'most directly'. According to Wikipedia the hamster later applied for a PhD at the University of Nijmegen. Geim developed a micro-fabricated adhesive mimicking a gecko lizard's sticky footpads. 'Singing mesh' – Terrence Tiller.

RED SPIDER MITE 'the feel of not to / feel it' – from 'In drear nighted December' by John Keats

SYCAMORE BARK Quotations are from *Paul Celan / Nelly Sachs: Correspondence*, translated by Christopher Clark (Sheep Meadow Press).

YARAK Three sentences of this poem are adapted from *Raptors of California* by Hans Peeters and Pam Peeters (University of California Press).

SEVEN SPRINGS OF OZLEWORTH The final two lines are adapted from Charles Tomlinson's poem 'In Arden' from *The Shaft* (Oxford University Press).

Acknowledgements

Birdbook: Farmland, Heathland, Mountain and Moorland (Sidekick Books); *Body*; *The Compass*; *The Dark Horse*; *Dear World* (Frosted Fire Press); *Huffington Post*; *Penning Perfumes* (Sabotage); *Poetry Archive*; *Poetry Review*; *The American Aesthetic*; *The Arts of Peace* (Two Rivers Press); *The Night of the Day* (Nine Arches Press); *Quadrant* (Australia); *The Rialto*; *The Tree Line: Poems for Trees, Woods and People* (Worple Press); *The Verb* (BBC Radio 3); *Wenlock Poetry Festival anthologies 2014, 2015, 2016* (Fair Acre Press); *The Wolf*.

'Husbandry', 'Lesson Three' and 'Yarak' were published in *The London Review of Books*.

Thanks are due to BBC Radio 5 Live for commissioning and broadcasting 'The Crowd'; Victoria Bennett for asking me to write a poem for *The Naked Muse* calendar in aid of the Juvenile Diabetes Research Foundation; Liverpool University for commissioning 'Their Son'; Poets and Players for commissioning 'The Discovery' to celebrate Manchester being the European City of Science for 2016.

Personal thanks to Siobhan Keenan, Ian Sansom, William Palmer and Gabriel and Edward; to Warwick University for a period of leave to help finish this book; to the Poetry Society (UK) for the Ted Hughes Award for New Work in Poetry; and to Brenda Tomlinson for reading the manuscript and choosing its title.